Frankie, Nancy and Rose on the Mountain

BY GAYLA McBRIDE EDWARDS
ILLUSTRATIONS BY VIKTORIIA DAVYDOVA

Illustrations and Cover Design by Viktoriia Davydova

ISBN: 978-0-578-33784-5

Library of Congress Cataloging-in-Publication Number:
TXu 2-281-987

Printed by Kindle Direct Publishing

gaylamcbrideedwardsbooks.wordpress.com

*This book is dedicated to
Frankie, Nancy and Rose.*

"If you're lucky enough to live on a mountain, you're lucky enough."

THIS BOOK is based on true events told by the grandchildren of Will and Cordelia Apple, who lived on Magazine Mountain in the Ozarks of Arkansas in the early 1900s. The stories are set on the mountain homestead in the year 1941. Although all are based on true happenings, parts of some of the chapters have been fictionalized by the author.

MAIN CHARACTERS and their ages in the book are:

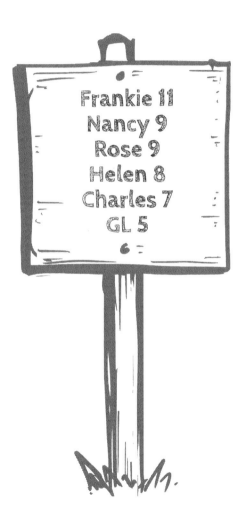

Frankie 11
Nancy 9
Rose 9
Helen 8
Charles 7
GL 5

Contents
Ahead

Prologue   10

Part One: Frankie

1 Getting There   19

2 Going to the Mailbox   27

3 Something in the Woods   35

4 Bob's Talent   38

5 Frankie Remembers the House-raising   43

6 Breaking the Churn   48

7 The Dare   51

Part Two: Nancy

1 STOPPING BY BARBER RIDGE ROAD   67

2 MYRTLE'S BLUE JAY   72

3 SHOOTING MARBLES
   (WHY PLOWING ONIONS WAS FUN)   79

4 THE OVERALLS   81

5 BUT JOY COMES IN THE MORNING   88

6 LEFT BEHIND   92

Part Three: Rose

1 GL PLANTS WATERMELON SEEDS   105

2 THE SPRING   109

3 BABY GOATS   111

4 THE SECRET   119

5 GL'S WATERMELON   125

6 MOTHER KNOWS BEST   130

Epilogue   135

Prologue
FRANKIE, NANCY AND ROSE

AT 2,753 FEET above sea level, beautiful Magazine Mountain boasts the highest point in Arkansas. Settlers began homesteading on the mountain in the mid to late 1800s. The Will Apple's Road Trail was the first road on Mt. Magazine and was named for the local farmer who peddled his outstanding fruits and vegetables throughout the valley below in the early 1900s. He hauled his famous produce from the mountaintop to the valley by horse and wagon using the path. Tour guides today point out to their attentive audience the historic home sites, wildflowers, different bird species, and old stone fences. The trail is also enjoyed by hikers, horseback riders, mountain bikers, and others looking for a place to get away from it all.

But to three young girls in Yell County, Arkansas in 1941, this path was simply part of the road to their Mama and Papa Apple's house, where their aunt, uncle, and fun-loving cousins also lived. To Frankie, Nancy, and Rose, their grandparents' farm on the mountain was the best place in the world.

Frankie and Nancy were sisters who lived at the foot of the mountain in the countryside town of Belleville. Rose, their cousin, lived alongside Shoal Creek beside the narrow winding road that led up the mountain face. Frankie was the oldest, having just turned eleven, with Nancy and Rose two years younger.

Frankie could often be found indoors, working on her movie star scrapbook of pictures cut from magazines. Nancy, a fierce competitor always full of energy, liked nothing better than playing games outdoors; in fact, the only thing that could entice her inside was a good book, as she loved to read.

Rose liked to play outside, but also enjoyed being indoors, cutting out pictures or making paper dolls.

Before going atop Mt. Magazine, Frankie and Nancy helped their parents prepare for the trip by loading the wagon with blankets and packing picnic lunches. They made sure to put in plenty of hay for the hard-working horses that would pull the wagon steadily up the crooked, steep cliffs of the mountain road. The girls had to get out of their cozy bed before dawn, when they went up on the mountain with their family, but they didn't mind this a bit, for a trip to the mountain meant good times spent playing with Rose, who would be there with her family, and their other cousins who lived on the mountain! It meant mothering the baby goats; eating from the orchards of delicious fruit that Will Apple was known to grow; and enjoying their Aunt Irene's sumptuous meals. To Rose, it meant time spent with all her cousins but especially with Nancy, for the two were "thick as thieves" when together— telling secrets and having the kind of adventures that only best friends and cousins can have.

Then when night came on the mountain after a long, full day of play, Frankie, Nancy, and Rose, alongside their other cousins, would go to sleep on pallets of soft blankets on the floor, while listening to the night sounds of frogs, crickets, owls and whippoorwills; and the jingling of bells on the goats moving on the hillside.

1
GETTING THERE

Tipper and Dollie came running, then stamped their hooves and shook their heads with what Frankie assumed was excitement for the trip. She knew that she and Nancy were plenty excited to head out with their parents to the mountain. The trip itself was always fun, and the anticipation of seeing and playing with their cousins gave them such a giddy feeling that they laughed uproariously about every little thing.

Nancy, glancing up to see the sun beginning to rise from the hillside, shouted to her family, "Hey, let's go, y'all, we're wasting daylight!"

Frankie and Nancy giggled uncontrollably at that, as Phoebe shook her head and Frank walked past ignoring them completely. Their daddy, Frank, hitched up Tipper and Dollie, and helped Nancy and Frankie into the wagon with their mother. Frank then climbed in himself, and they started the day's journey.

After a while Frank pointed out the new and pretty Spring Lake, where some of his good friends and the other men working for the WPA had beautifully created the 82-acre lake and dam, along with a bridge over it for people to stroll across. But Frankie and Nancy were not even tempted to ask to walk across the dam today—their cousins were waiting!

After riding for another long while, they came to the landmark that people called 'the Old Gum Tree' which was a black gum tree that stood between the forks of the road. A large wooden table had been built circling around the trunk of the old tree. People wrote messages on pieces of paper, then stuck them on nails which had been hammered into the table. Frank let Frankie and Nancy leap from the wagon to look at the messages. *The Jamie Laster family will be having a picnic at Spring Lake today at noon,* a lined page written in neat cursive announced. *Our coon dog is missing,* another page proclaimed, *He answers to Bo.* Frankie and Nancy told each other they would watch closely for Bo as they rode, and they did, too, but they never saw any coon dogs at all.

"Look, girls, that's where your daddy went to school. And he taught there, too. It's where Rose goes to church, you know."

Frankie and Nancy dutifully glanced at the one-room schoolhouse which was also Rose's church, even though their mother pointed it out every time they came.

On and on the horses trotted, carrying them a little closer to Mama and Papa Apple's with each hoofbeat.

After a long while of watching the trees pass slowly by, Frankie's bottom began to feel very tired of riding. Nancy kept shuffling on the seat, messing up the blanket that their mother had spread for them to sit on. When Frankie, very politely, asked her to stop, saying, "Nancy, be still, please," her sister just frowned at her. Then, when she said it again, but this time a little louder, Nancy stuck out her tongue at her!

"Mother!" Frankie started, but then saw they were nearing Shoal Creek!

Frank Apple pulled the horses to a halt, and Frankie and Nancy scrambled out to play in the water, while the horses rested for a bit and had a drink. The girls followed the creek a way to see what they could see.

Frankie and Nancy came to a small waterfall, and gingerly made their way down it. The pretty, innocent-looking green moss that covered parts of the rocks was deceptively slick as lard, the girls knew, and they carefully made their choices of stepping stones.

Continuing on, Frankie came upon a beautiful blue and silver lizard sunning on a rock. She attempted to catch it to see if its tail would fall off, but the dozing lizard woke up very fast when it saw a hand coming toward it, and was gone in an instant.

When Frank and Phoebe called the girls—too soon, Frankie thought—to come back to the wagon to continue on their trip, Frankie stood rooted at the spot to look out on Shoal Creek one more time.

It's the most beautiful place I ever saw, she marveled to herself as she took in the crystal-clear creek surrounded by rolling green hills—with majestic Mt. Magazine, their destination, beaconing in the distance.

Frankie began to picture Shirley Temple making her next movie here in all this prettiness. As she was trying to decide which rock Shirley would be standing on in the introduction, and whether Shirley should be lost or maybe escaping from someone mean and cruel, she heard her sister's exasperated call.

"*C'mon*, Frankie!"

Nancy was already halfway back to the wagon, so Frankie reluctantly made her way to join her family.

As the good horses led them on, Frank began humming, then singing a hymn. Frankie and Nancy, and their mother too, joined in, "I'll… fly *away*, oh glo-ory, I'll…fly away…" then Frank sang deeply, Frankie's favorite part, "in the *morn*-in'…" They sang more hymns, with Frankie and Nancy taking turns deciding which ones to sing, and the time went by quickly.

"There's Old Man Squires' place!" Nancy and Frankie shouted at the same time.

Frankie and Nancy always wanted to have

their picnic lunch under the big shade trees by the stream just past Old Man Squire's place. Frankie didn't even know who Old Man Squire *was*, but she always looked forward to seeing his house, anyway, because it meant lunch time was coming up.

The leftover breakfast biscuits her mother had packed, with a thick slice of salty, smoked ham between each one, made for a pleasant meal, but a quick one as they had miles left to travel that day.

The next stop was the little community called Millard. There was a store there, small but with foodstuffs and some hardware items for mountain dwellers who might need a few things but couldn't make the long trip down the mountain to town. Frank again watered the horses and let them rest, and Frank and Phoebe visited with folks at the store for a little while.

Then, it was time to go up the steep part of the mountain, with its S-shaped curves and twists the rest of the way. The road went up so sharply, Frankie was afraid the horses were going to fall backward onto them in the wagon, and she told her family that a few times, until they all told her to stop being silly. Of course, Tipper and Dollie always got them there just fine, so Frankie knew it *was* silly to worry about it, but she did every time anyway.

Frankie just couldn't wait to get there, to see her cousins and aunt and uncle, who all lived with her grandparents on the mountain, and of course she was also eager to see her grandparents, whom she called Mama Apple and Papa Apple, too. School had let out for the summer a week ago, and Frankie and Nancy had been counting down the days until they could stay at Mama and Papa Apple's. Their cousin Rose who lived close by would be there, and of course the cousins who lived there—Helen, Charles, and GL—along with their parents, Lee and Irene. Frankie and Nancy would ride home, come next week or maybe the next, with Papa Apple or Uncle Lee as they peddled their produce down the valley.

And they could come back lots of times through the summer, too, following this same routine, Frankie thought happily.

The horses flew over a bump in the road and Frankie's bottom went up and came down hard, bringing her thoughts back to the present. They were almost to Mama and Papa Apple's clearing!

Frankie sat up straight as her younger sister grabbed her hand and bounced on the seat in excitement for the day.

2

Going to the Mailbox

Frankie glanced up to find her grandmother smiling, rocking gently back and forth in her old oak rocking chair. When Nancy and her cousins played games outside, Frankie often chose to stay inside with Mama Apple. Frankie had lived with Mama and Papa Apple for six months when she was two years old, while her mother was very sick, and she'd had a special bond with her grandmother from that time on. Frankie liked nothing better than to sit by her grandmother's side as she wrote letters or embroidered.

Frankie had recently learned to play chords on

the old organ that sat regally in the room alongside the rocking chair. What made her grandmother look so pleased as she sat rocking today was Frankie's organ-playing, and Frankie sat up straighter with pride as she played on.

"Frankie Lou, I believe you have a special talent for that organ," her grandmother began when Frankie finally stopped playing and stood up, stretching. "I don't wonder but what you will be playing at church one of these days, when—" Nancy burst through the door then, so Frankie didn't find out just when Mama Apple thought she might play the organ for church.

"Come on, Frankie, we're going to pick peaches!" Nancy shouted.

Nancy knew that Frankie especially liked the peach orchard. The peach trees were so pretty! *And the orchard even **smells** pretty*, Frankie thought to herself sillily. Of course, she enjoyed *eating* the sweet, aromatic fruit, too. Frankie was grateful to her sister for coming for her, and she hurried to the door to go with Nancy to the peach orchard.

"After you bring the peaches in, girls, we'll go to the mailbox," Mama Apple called after them, and

Frankie whooped a cheer of happiness at this, for she loved to go to the mailbox.

Someone walked the trail to the mailbox nearly every day. It seemed like an all-day trip to Frankie. Mama Apple had told her once, when she'd asked, that it was only about two miles as the crow flies.

But, Frankie contradicted Mama Apple secretly, *the mailbox is almost to where you can see Shoal Creek streaming down the mountain, and that's a considerable distance.*

As they crossed the road to the peach orchard, Frankie frowned, trying to calculate the miles.

First, there was the sandy road…they would take off their shoes and carry them on that part… then they'd start up the path that was rugged and steep, cut deep into rocks and roots—from wear and tear and water erosion, Mama Apple had told her.

Wasn't that two miles already?

Then they reached the part of the trail that seemed to go straight up. That part seemed a bit scary to Frankie, although Nancy called it fun.

That was…hmm…another mile and a half.

Before arriving at the mailbox, they were on

level road again and glad to be out of the rocks for the last part of the hike. Then, of course, there were the miles to go back home, sometimes with letters in hand, as their prize.

Frankie was getting confused with trying to add up miles and finally concluded that Mama Apple was probably right about how far it was, since they *were* always back before dinner.

The children picked peaches until they had filled up the basket Aunt Irene had sent with them. Then they picked more and sat on the ground eating peaches for a long while. Peach juice dribbled down Charles' face, and Frankie thought about laughing at him, but then she felt some juice running down her own chin and decided not to point out Charles' peach juice.

Why are Papa Apple's fruits and vegetables so good, Frankie wondered.

Besides the pretty peaches, the grapes were enormous—like the grapes Joshua and Caleb found as spies in the Bible, Frankie reckoned—the onions were exceptionally sweet, and the watermelons? Why, people came from all over when it was watermelon season to ask to buy them, and they'd say things like, 'Will, you grow the best watermelons of any in

Arkansas.' Uncle Lee had told her once when she'd asked that the mountain air and soil up here made the crops better, but her mother had said that it was just the loving care they put into growing them.

Frankie didn't consider the matter for long. Glancing up from her thought of it being the air, or soil, or loving care that made the crops grow so well, Frankie saw Mama Apple waving to them to come to the house. It was time to go to the mailbox!

When they got to the porch, Mama Apple took the peaches and started into the house to set them down.

"Grandma, can we go by ourselves today?" Rose called.

No doubt thinking of being able to peel peaches and help Aunt Irene with the baking, Mama Apple said that would be all right.

Thus, the children started on their expedition.

When they reached the end of the road, the children stopped, as they always did, to put their shoes on before stepping into the forest to walk its trail…all of them, that is, except Charles, whose feet were used to the rocks and brush, and were much admired by the others for their toughness.

When they got to the very steep part of the trail,

they had a race to see who could get to the top first. Nancy won, as usual, but Rose was right on her heels. Frankie trailed behind them all, but she didn't care. She placed her feet carefully, choosing the sturdiest rocks to plant them on and the strongest limbs to catch as she went up, up, up.

Finally, all the children were at the top, and continued on the last leg of the trip to the mailbox. There was a letter to Mama Apple from Aunt Jimmy and Uncle Willie, which made them all feel happy because Mama Apple would be proud to get it when they got back.

They started down the steep part, not racing this time but everybody being careful, not wanting to take a tumble down the brushy hillside. When the children were down the hill and on the path again, Helen stopped and stood very still.

"What is it?" Frankie asked her, but Helen just shushed her with a finger to her lips.

They all stood there a minute, not knowing what they were listening for, then Helen shrugged and started walking again.

"I thought I heard something," she said by way of explanation.

They hadn't walked but a few more steps, though, when Frankie thought she heard a noise, too.

"Stop a minute," she said, and the children went through it again—listening, then shrugging and walking.

They did that two more times before they started walking very fast and not talking much. Frankie guessed that the others were thinking the same thought she was, though. Uncle Lee and Papa Apple had never seen one or even signs of one, but they had heard talk from people at church and at the Millard store that there was a *panther* in these woods!

3

SOMETHING IN THE WOODS

Frankie kept arguing in her mind about it, telling herself that Mama Apple wouldn't have let them go by themselves if she thought there might be a panther—but then, that man at the store the other day had sounded so certain that he had heard one…

Charles gulped and pointed. There appeared two tiny glowing circles of light in the dark green shades of the forest. They looked almost like… animal eyes…staring at its prey, Frankie was forced to consider, and she shivered in spite of the warmth of the afternoon.

The children started running, jumping, hopping and sometimes tripping over stumps, rocks and huge oak roots. Frankie was too scared to look behind her, but she didn't really need to, anyway, because Nancy was looking back with almost every step, so Frankie kept an eye on her sister's face for any additional alarm in her expression.

When they finally jogged out of the brush and onto the level road on the last stretch home, the children all started running at full speed. They bounded up the porch steps and went into the house panting and holding their sides from running so hard.

Frankie suddenly remembered the letter and, still puffing and panting, but now more from leftover excitement than the escape from possibly being eaten, handed it to Mama Apple. She noticed how wrinkled Uncle Willie's letter was from her clenching it so tightly in her hand.

Astonishingly, Mama Apple and Aunt Irene must have just thought they had been having a race for fun because they didn't say a word about them coming in breathing so hard like that, although Mama Apple did look at the wrinkled-up letter for a minute, and then laid it on the table to try to press it out flat. Aunt Irene asked if they would go bring in some wood and load the oven so she could start supper, and everybody had kind of caught their breath by then, so they headed out the door.

And there they saw him!

He was laying under the big oak tree, right beneath the old wooden swing! He raised his head to look at them when they came out.

It wasn't a *panther*, though—it was just a scraggly, mud-covered, thin, sad-eyed *dog*!

4

Bob's Talent

"He must have followed us almost all the way from the mailbox," Helen surmised.

"He sure is ugly," GL noted.

Frankie was already at the swing, though, holding out her hand for him to sniff, and Nancy had headed straight into the kitchen to find a biscuit to give him. Charles ran to fill up a bowl of water to bring their new friend that wasn't a panther, and the stray lapped it almost all up. He ate all the biscuit and some chicken, too. Aunt Irene, who loved all animals, said right away that they could keep Bob, whom GL named after another dog they had had one time. Bob didn't have a short, bobbed tail like the dog before, but that didn't matter to GL, he still was partial to the name.

After a bath followed by some good dinners every day, and a lot of tummy rubs and kind words from all the family, Bob started following the other dogs around and getting to be friends with them. He was interested in everything, and easily learned how to fetch and return the baseball Nancy threw for him.

But the talent that made him kind of famous, at least among everyone who lived on the mountain, and now that Frankie thought about it, even some people in the valley, was herding the hogs.

Bob's talent for herding was discovered when Mama Apple was bringing the cows into the barn one day. Bob jumped right in and started nipping and racing around them and had them in the barn lickety-split. Mama Apple said she never saw anything like it.

Herding the *hogs*, though, was by far his most showy craft. Bob turned out to be the envy of everyone who saw him round them up and bring them in, when the leaves changed color and it was time to go get the sows from the woods. Neighbors from miles away came just to watch Bob do his work!

It was a challenging job for any dog. Papa Apple always let the sows out of their pen to run free in the woods through the spring and summer, so that they could feast on the nuts, roots, bulbs and other goodness of the forest floor. The contented pigs raised their litters of piglets in hidden nesting places they found in the woods. In the fall Papa Apple and Uncle Lee would entice the pigs out with corn nubbins, then have the best dogs drive them home and into their pen. The hogs would be fed corn in the months remaining before butchering time, so that the family could have firm and tasty ham, bacon and salt meat in the winter.

With Bob's leadership, the hogs were rounded up in no time, grunting and darting through the woods, with a resolute Bob and the other dogs behind them. For their hardship in having to come in from the woods like that, Papa Apple always had a full feeding trough waiting in the pen for the pigs' treat; after Bob had made sure the last pig was in the pen, he led the other dogs to Papa Apple and Uncle Lee to wait for their words of praise and bucket of cold fresh water that they knew would be waiting for them.

From time to time, some people would offer Papa Apple money for Bob, and Frankie's heart always fluttered a bit whenever she heard them, although Papa Apple just laughed a little each time and told them no.

"Well, this dog sure repaid us for being kind to him when he needed it," Aunt Irene said of Bob one evening as the family sat on the porch together after dinner.

Bob wagged his tail and looked into Frankie's eyes, and her heart filled with love.

Still, Frankie never forgot that day coming home from the mailbox when she and her cousins had thought Bob was a panther.

5
Frankie Remembers
the House-raising

Mama Apple's eyebrows raised, then came a small smile, followed by a shake of her head; once she even laughed out loud. She was reading the letter that had come in the mailbox today, from Aunt Jimmy and Uncle Willie.

"Mama Apple, tell me about Maxine! What about Maxine?" Frankie begged, when at last her grandmother finished reading.

Mama Apple handed Frankie the letter to read for herself, but said, "Maxine is doing real well, Uncle Willie says. She made all A's on her report card, and she's learning to play the piano from a lady at church."

Maxine was Frankie's oldest cousin, one year older than her, to be exact. She and Frankie used to have a lot of fun playing together at Mama and Papa Apple's until she, along with her parents (who were Frankie's Uncle Willie and Aunt Jimmy) and her brother Donny and baby sister Mona, moved to Kansas.

Frankie began reading and, sure enough, Maxine had made all A's and was learning piano. But when Frankie got to the part about the slide Maxine helped her Daddy make out of a board for little Mona, she felt like laughing and crying at the same time because she remembered when she and Maxine made the same slides at the house-raising when they were little. Frankie wandered out to the front porch with the letter and sat on the top step as her mind drifted back to the day of the house-raising…

* * *

"Frankie Lou, help me with this."

Maxine was walking toward her, lugging a board that was three times her height. All their aunts and uncles and all their cousins were at Mama and

Papa Apple's for a house raising, which, her mother had explained to Frankie, meant that Mama and Papa Apple were getting a new house and all their children were helping to build it.

"I've got an idea," Maxine continued as she dropped the board and looked at Frankie, grinning. "I thought of a way to keep the little kids busy so you and I can go down the road and pick muscadines by ourselves."

Maxine had just turned seven years old, and Frankie was six, so they felt quite mature, next to the "little kids," just two, three, and four years old. Maxine was quite resourceful and had some very good ideas a lot of times, so Frankie was all ears.

Maxine took her cousin over to the house being constructed and pointed up to one of the holes in the wall where the window was soon to be.

"Now, you hold this board," she said, thrusting the end of it into Frankie's stomach, "I'm going up there."

They then proceeded to make a slide going from the soon-to-be windowsill to the ground.

Nancy, Rose, and Donny had gathered around by this time to see what they were doing. Rose slid down first, screaming with glee. Nancy and Donny soon followed suit. Frankie and Maxine exchanged knowing looks, feeling very clever about the success of Maxine's good idea.

Maxine decided that, before going to ask Mama Apple for a bucket to put their muscadines in, maybe they should try out the slide themselves, just to make sure it wasn't wobbly or anything, before they left the little ones on their own.

"That's good thinking!" Frankie said to her cousin.

No muscadines ever got picked that day! Maxine and Frankie had so much fun going down that slide that they began to put more long boards through other window holes, until they had a veritable amusement park of slides. They had tall slides and not so tall slides, narrow slides and one wide enough for two kids to go down at the same time… Maxine and Frankie were sorry when Uncle Willie told them it was time to put the windows in, so get those boards out of there.

However, their Mama and Papa Apple had a nice new house that day, and they were glad of that.

* * *

Frankie sat on the step for a long while, being nostalgic. She thought about how lucky she was to have her built-in, forever friends—her cousins.

When Mama Apple called through the screen door to see if Frankie wanted to write Maxine a letter to put in with the one she was writing for Aunt Jimmy and Uncle Willie, Frankie readily agreed. She filled up a whole page, front and back, with news for Maxine. She ended it by asking Maxine if she remembered when they made the slides a long time ago.

Then she signed her name, handed it to Mama Apple, and ran outside to find her cousins to see if they wanted to play a game or go to the spring or something.

6

BREAKING THE CHURN

Frankie had never seen her cousin Helen mad before, but right before her eyes she saw her… clenching a hammer, pounding on Mama Apple's churn, and breaking it into bits!

Frankie was afraid to approach her, such a look of fierce determination was on Helen's face, but she wanted to be a proper friend to her usually good-natured cousin, so she courageously made her way almost right to her and said gently, "Helen, what happened? What's the matter?" Helen looked up, and Frankie truly thought she had not even seen her there.

"Huh?" Helen said, hammer up and at the ready.

"What's the matter?" Frankie repeated. "Why are you breaking Grandma's churn?"

Helen broke out in a huge grin.

"Oh, this!" she said as she began laughing.

She laughed and laughed until tears were rolling down her cheeks. Now, *Frankie* was the one feeling mad, at not knowing what her cousin was so gleeful about.

"It's for the…it's for the chickens!" Helen gasped.

Frankie frowned as Helen kept on until she got all her laughing out. Her eyes still watery from the laughing tears, Helen finally became serious and explained to Frankie that the churn was an old one that was broken beyond repair, and Grandma had sent her to break it up and crush the pieces to feed to the chickens.

Helen patiently went on to tell Frankie that the crushed pieces were what Grandma called grit and when the chickens swallow it, it goes into the gizzard—a strong, tough body part—and helps grind the feed they eat to get it ready for digestion.

"Chicken don't have teeth, so they need the extra help," Helen continued.

Frankie remembered then that Mama Apple fed the chickens baked, crumbled eggshells sometimes, but she had never thought about why her grandmother did that. She asked Helen, and Helen said yes, it served the same purpose, and that it also makes the chickens' eggshells harder.

Frankie stood there for a minute more watching Helen pound with her hammer, then she took off running for the house. It was Helen's turn to wonder, now, about Frankie.

"I'll be right back!" Frankie turned around to yell to her.

And, after Frankie had asked her grandmother for a hammer, she ran back to help her cousin pound the crockery.

7

THE DARE

Dinner on the mountain was at noon each day, supper in the evening. Both meals were resplendent with Aunt Irene's fluffy biscuits; ham, beef or fried chicken; a huge assortment of vegetables; crispy fried potatoes; white or red-eye gravy; big bowls of berries; and almost always, to Frankie's delight, her aunt's mouth-watering huckleberry cobbler.

Uncle Lee and Papa Apple came for dinner when Aunt Irene and Mama Apple struck the dinner bell. The bell hung from a tree branch in front of the tater house, which was the small building used for storing potatoes, onions, apples and other of the season's growth, so that it wouldn't freeze in the cold winter months. The large cast-iron bell was hit with a steel rod that was propped up beside it for that purpose.

Before they came in for dinner, Uncle Lee and Papa Apple drew bucket upon bucket of water from the well, for the horses they had been using to plow. Frankie was amazed at how much water those horses could drink after a hard morning's work!

Papa Apple always sat at the head of the dinner table and said the blessing. He had a big mustache, and he bent his head way over when he prayed, so, although Frankie enjoyed the rhythm of the blessing, she never understood a word he was saying. But she never worried about it, because she wasn't the one he was talking to, anyway. It was fun to sit with Nancy, and Rose and the other cousins, on the bench between the table and the windows, although they had to remember not to lean back, or they might fall backwards right through the screen on the open window!

After dinner, Uncle Lee would go out on the front porch and turn one of the straight back wooden chairs over to transform it into a recliner, then take a nap before going back with Papa Apple and the good, faithful horses to work in the crops until supper.

When all the aunts, uncles and cousins were over for dinner, the kids had to wait until after the grown-ups had eaten to have their meal. Frankie and Nancy and their cousins played outside until the adults had had their fill of the good food and conversation. Then, it was their turn to sit at the table, on the long bench reserved for the kids, and enjoy the plenteous food.

Sometimes while they were waiting outside, Frankie smelled those wonderful smells coming through the open windows and peeked in impatiently, although she was mostly content to play and wait, along with her sister and cousins, for their turn.

But the day Charles noticed her looking in the window and dared her, and she didn't ignore him, things turned into a heck of a mess for Frankie.

Frankie was tired of horseshoes—she wasn't very good at them anyway, and golly, she was hungry. Those smells! There's nothing like the smell of fried chicken to make you even hungrier when you're already hungry to begin with. Frankie was frowning and looking in at the grown-ups, who had just sat down and were starting to gobble up big bites of dinner, when Charles burst out, "Dare ya to go ask if you can eat at the grown-up table."

She should have just laughed at him then, and gone back to playing horseshoes, Frankie knew, but instead she retorted, "Maybe I will."

Those three words—*maybe I will*—were what got her into the heck of a mess. As soon as Frankie said them, she regretted it.

Rose, waiting her turn at throwing the horseshoe, turned to say, "Well, Frankie, you should ask!"

Nancy, who was shaking her head with disgust at her poor throw, turned from the game to chime in, "Do it! Go ask Mama Apple!"

Frankie tried making excuses.

"Well, they've already sat down now," she started, but Helen answered, "Only just now, though… Mother's just passing the biscuits around."

I can't say I want to play horseshoes instead— they've already heard me complain about playing, a couple of times, Frankie thought.

When she couldn't think of a single good excuse, Frankie started feeling braver.

*Maybe I **should** ask to eat with the grown-ups.*

Why not? I'm eleven now, after all! This might turn out to be the perfect day!

Frankie smiled to herself.

She was feeling quite confident now, and strode into the dining room where her mother glanced up to ask, "Frankie, did you need something?"

"No, I just wanted to ask if I might sit at the table to eat now, instead of waiting for the *kids*."

When she said that, though, everybody stopped what they were doing to stare at her. For a long moment, no one said anything, but Mama Apple pulled a chair over to the table and motioned her to it. Then, everyone started eating and talking and passing bowls of food around again.

Frankie breathed a sigh of relief that the awkwardness was over.

Sitting in a chair is nice, Frankie thought to herself.

But as soon as she thought it, she knew that she missed sitting on the long bench by the window, jostling elbows with her cousins.

Frankie quietly filled her plate from the heaping bowls and platters passed her way, and decided to make the most of the refined conversation that she was likely to be a part of at the adult table.

Papa Apple and Uncle Lee were telling her daddy and Uncle Emery about the bumper crop of corn they were having this year, but, they went on to say, the goldarn weevils were getting into the green beans. Then they started regaling each other with stories of how to get rid of weevils.

Frankie turned her attention to Aunt Irene, who was asking Aunt Rosa her opinion of the curtains at church, and whether she ought to bring it up to the pastor that maybe she could make some new curtains; but would that hurt the feelings of so and so who had made the curtains that were there now? Her mother and Mama Apple and her aunts were all completely wrapped up in the topic, but Frankie found it hard to get interested in the curtains, or the weevil stories either, for that matter. It was all… well, boring.

She began to wonder how the horseshoe game was going. Then Frankie realized she hadn't heard the sounds of horseshoes clanking or her cousins and sister laughing, in a while, and looking out the large open windows, she didn't see them anywhere.

An awful idea hit her: They must have gone to see the baby goats! Frankie wondered sadly who was holding her little Annie now, and if Annie was getting comfortable with them and forgetting about her.

"Daddy, could you please pass the corn on the cob?" she finally cut into the conversation.

You would have thought I'd asked for a hundred dollars! Frankie confided later to Nancy.

Her mother said, "Why, Frankie, didn't you already have two ears of corn?"

Uncle Lee began to laugh at her, the others joining in.

Frankie's face burned as she determinedly took the biggest ear of corn from the platter passed to her and chomped down on it. Scarcely tasting it in her embarrassment, Frankie reckoned to herself that adults didn't keep eating corn on the cob and pile up stacks of corncobs by their plates, deciding then to turn it into a corn on the cob eating contest.

At least she could have first choice of dessert (along with the other adults at the table, of course). Imagine Frankie's horror when Aunt Irene brought in the huckleberry cobbler and pitcher of cream, only to hear all the grown-ups start saying, "Oh, I couldn't possibly!" and "Irene, we can't eat another bite!"

Frankie most definitely could have eaten another

bite, and another and another, of Aunt Irene's sweet buttery cobbler with cream poured over it.

But she grudgingly agreed, "Oh, no, none for me either, Aunt Irene."

Frankie watched longingly as Aunt Irene opened the warmer oven and placed it back inside, then set the lonely-looking pitcher of cream on the counter.

Uncle Lee was already calling out the door for the kids to come eat. Mama Apple asked if Frankie wanted to sit and embroider with her.

Usually there was nothing Frankie would rather do than work on the doily she had been making with the pretty daisy and butterfly design. It was made with real fabric instead of the pieces of feed sacks which were generally used for all sewing projects, and she had been looking forward to maybe finishing it today. Somehow, though, it didn't seem that she should be working on it now, it seemed like she should be joining Nancy and her cousins on the bench to laugh, and eat all the corn on the cob they wanted, and talk about interesting things—like baby goats, or whether there were bobcats in the woods or not.

Frankie miserably stitched on her doily and listened to her cousins' laughter from the dining

room until Mama Apple said to go check to see if the kids were finished, and have them start the dishes. It was Frankie and Helen's turn to do dishes, Frankie remembered, and she was so ready to have that awful mealtime erased from her mind that she could hardly wait to get started.

Nancy and her cousins were just starting on their bowlfuls of cobbler, still warm from the warmer oven, with sweet cream filled to the brim of each mouth-watering bowl. Frankie told Helen to come get her when she was done, then went slowly back to her embroidery.

At last, the laughter from the dining room died down, and Helen stuck her head in to say she was ready to do the dishes.

"I'll bet eating with the grown-ups was fun," Helen said wistfully as she plunged her hands into the dishwater.

"Well, to be honest, I missed sitting on the bench with you and everybody else," Frankie admitted.

"You *did?*"

"Yeah," Frankie grinned.

Helen stopped scrubbing a plate to look at her older cousin for a long moment.

"Frankie Lou, we missed you too," she said.

"Charles said two times that he wished he'd never made that dare to you. And Rose cried a little when she said we probably wouldn't ever get to eat with you again at the kids' table."

That made Frankie feel a lot better, and when Helen suggested they have another piece of cobbler after they finished the dishes, Frankie didn't tell her she hadn't even had a taste yet; she just agreed. It was the best of Aunt Irene's cobblers, Frankie decided later as they licked their spoons, that she had ever had.

The next time all the aunts and uncles and cousins were there, Frankie worried about the upcoming meal. Would the grown-ups expect her at their table? Would she have to eat with the adults forever more, and be bored and say no to dessert, all because of a stupid dare she accepted one time?

But no one called her in from the front yard to come to dinner with the adults (and she wasn't even tempted to peek in the window). Instead, Frankie trooped in gladly with her sister and cousins when the adults had finished their meal.

Frankie, moreover, was the one who suggested they have a corn on the cob eating contest…which she won!

Part Two

Nancy

STOPPING BY
BARBER RIDGE ROAD

From Nancy and Frankie's house in Belleville to Mama and Papa Apple's on the mountain was seventeen miles. It took much of the day to get there. Usually Frank and Phoebe, their mother and daddy, chose the route that led by Spring Lake, then the old gum tree, and Shoal Creek, which was a very nice way; but sometimes they went what their mother called the other way, which was a road that led through the town of Havana, instead.

Nancy liked best going "the other way," because sometimes they stopped at McBride's General Store, which was fun; and it was that road that led by the Samuel J. Barber place on Barber Ridge Road, so

Nancy got to see where the *Rural Record* was printed. Frank always stopped there in the sandy lot for the horses to rest, and Phoebe unfailingly reminded the girls that this was where the newspaper was produced!

Today was shaping up to be an especially good day for Nancy, because she overheard her mother tell her daddy, why don't we go the other way today.

Sure enough, they stopped at McBride's, and Nancy and Frankie were given a nickel each to choose from the wide array of bins lining the candy counter. Nancy picked out three long sticks of hard candy of different flavors and opened one right away to pass the time while riding. Frankie chose taffy and was given five pieces in a small brown sack, which she politely passed around to share with her mother, daddy and Nancy.

On and on they rode, until they neared Barber Ridge Road and their next stop. Nancy sat up a little straighter as Tipper and Dollie, remembering that this was where they would get their next drink and a rest, trotted gaily into the lot of the newspaper office.

The Rural Record newspaper was read by all who lived in the valley towns in the shadow of Mt.

Magazine. At their house, as in others across the valley, it was always a special day when the mailman brought the Record with all the community news.

To think, the pages of that wonderful newspaper all were brought into existence right here! Nancy felt privileged to see the building where it was faithfully developed each week.

She could hardly believe it, though, when her daddy said, "What do you say we go inside and see how this newspaper-printing business works?"

He was actually talking to her mother, Nancy knew, but that didn't stop her, and Frankie, too, from shouting, "Yes, yes, can we, Daddy? Can we?"

Phoebe smiled and answered, "Not without shoes, young lady," so Nancy quickly pulled her socks and saddle shoes back on, then jumped from the wagon to join Frankie, who had never even taken hers off. Frank and Phoebe were already on the porch, knocking at the door of the newspaper office to ask if it would be all right. Nancy knew the answer was yes when her father, grinning, turned to the girls and beckoned them onto the porch.

Inside the little building, the two Barber sisters, tall and slender with shiny dark hair, smiled as they showed Nancy and Frankie how they aligned tiny rubber ABCs in a large metal block to spell words, sentences, paragraphs…stories! Mr. Barber then led them across the room where a big machine whirled the newspapers into being. Nancy stood watching, so mesmerized by the process that she did not catch much of what the gracious Mr. Barber told them about it. She came out of her daze only when she heard her daddy say thank you to Mr. Barber.

Nancy thanked him, too, then snuck one more look at the Barber sisters as she followed the rest of her family out into the bright sunlight. Their dresses did not look to be made from feed sacks, and in fact were maybe even store-bought. They seemed perfectly content to be arranging the words of the stories that people all over the valley would soon be reading. The little newspaper building was across the road from their house, in the cool of the shade. They didn't have to be out in the hot sun hoeing or picking cotton, as Nancy's family did at home. Why, Nancy didn't even *see* a cotton field in those hills.

And, although they never knew it, the Barber sisters became Nancy's role models.

2

MYRTLE'S BLUE JAY

"*Pleeease, Helen*…I'll help you with your chores, you know I will…please, let's go…"

Nancy wanted, more than anything, for Helen and Charles to walk with her to their neighbors' house to see their friends Claud and Myrtle. Charles was willing, but Helen…well, Helen was just making excuses, Nancy thought, scowling.

Claud and Myrtle Hignight's parents were Monroe and Lizzie. Nancy had never been there, but she knew the family because they were at Mama and Papa Apple's sometimes, and they always helped the family when they gathered in the fall to make sorghum molasses from the sweet sugarcane that grew in thick stalks by the woods.

Myrtle Hignight had recently raised a baby blue jay that had fallen from its nest. The last time Myrtle had walked over to see them, the blue jay had followed her all the way. It pecked at little pieces of bread that she held out, and flitted around her almost like a puppy would do! Claud told them that the bird even roosted at the foot of Myrtle's bed every night. Nancy had been very much intrigued by Myrtle's pet and from that day on had wanted to go see it. She wanted to know if Myrtle had named it yet, too, because she had a name in mind if not.

"Well, *maybe* I'll go with you—if you play croquet with me tomorrow."

Nancy didn't tell Helen that she would have been very happy to play croquet, anyway.

"*Yes*!" Nancy huffed instead, frowning at her cousin but smiling with delight on the inside. "We can play for as long as you want!"

And at that Helen said the magic words: "All right."

As they headed into the dense woods, Nancy began to see why Helen had trepidations about going. The children struggled for what seemed many miles through brush and thorns, and over huge rocks and cliffs. Nancy knew they weren't lost because Helen and Charles knew all the territory on the mountain, but still she was starting to feel hopeless of ever getting there. Finally, though, they reached the barbed wire fence and huge clearing, and the house was in sight. The children knocked on the back door and Mrs. Hignight called to them to come on in.

They stepped into the kitchen and saw Myrtle's mother standing at the table, squeezing a cloth bag. Nancy tried to decide what she was making. She breathed in deeply for clues. It smelled like soured buttermilk, she decided, but with a whiff of teacake smell mixed in with it. Mrs. Hignight motioned Nancy up to peer inside, and she saw that the bag was full of thick milky-white cream. Mrs. Hignight kept on kneading the bag, like it was dough, while she exchanged pleasantries with her young callers.

"Cottage cheese?" Nancy finally ventured, even though it wasn't lumpy like cottage cheese and didn't have the right smell for it at all.

Mrs. Hignight smiled at her and said no, but that it *was* a kind of cheese called quark; they could have a taste of it in a bit. Mrs. Hignight told them that she had learned how to make quark from her mother, who had learned from *her* mother in Germany, where she was born and grew up before coming to America.

Mrs. Hignight then sent them out to find Claud and Myrtle.

Nancy, Helen and Charles could see their friends across the way in the truck plot of peas, helping their dad plow. When kind Mr. Hignight saw the children walking that way, he motioned for Myrtle and Claud to go on and visit with them.

Nancy spotted the blue jay right away! It fluttered near Myrtle, took off to soar above the treetops, then flew back down to perch on a low branch, where it chirped and cocked its head at the children. Claud went into the kitchen to get a piece of bread, then they tore off tiny pieces to give to the bird.

"Her name is Tillie," Myrtle told the children.

Nancy decided not to mention that she'd had a good name picked out.

When they had been there for a while, Tillie became more used to the newcomers and apparently began feeling comfortable enough to start in on her 'mischief' as Myrtle called it. The bird started finding odds and ends and then flying over to where they were sitting, to plant them…in the children's hair!

First it was a tiny pine cone, then a piece of ribbon deposited into Myrtle's hair. A little while later, Tillie lightly dropped onto *Nancy's* head and left a tiny acorn. Soon the bird began spreading her treasures out amongst them all. Myrtle just rolled her eyes, but the rest of them found it pretty funny.

When Tillie decided to alight on Nancy's knee, Nancy gasped with delight. She took slow soft breaths so that the beautiful creature might choose to stay a while. When Tillie turned her little head up to look with bright black eyes right into Nancy's, she held her breath altogether.

The bird soon left to take up its usual spot on Myrtle's shoulder, but Nancy held on to the memory of the wild yet delicate creature resting on her knee, trusting her enough to look into her eyes.

Remembering the cheese with the funny name, Nancy suggested they go in to tell Mrs. Hignight good-bye before they left. Sure enough, when they knocked on the door and told her thank you for letting them come over, she offered them a taste of it.

Mrs. Hignight spooned out a little into three cups, one for each of them. It wasn't like any cheese Nancy ever knew of. On her tongue it was sweet but tangy, even a little sour, and was the smooth thickness of homemade ice cream. Nancy decided she liked it very much.

They told Mrs. Hignight thank you again, then started their trek back to Mama and Papa Apple's.

Going back didn't seem to take as long as getting there had, with Myrtle's blue jay and the cheese that didn't taste like cheese occupying Nancy's thoughts.

She was sure glad she had talked Helen into going to the Hignight's.

And I get to play croquet tomorrow, too! Nancy thought with a sly smile.

At dinner that night, after Aunt Irene asked how Mrs. Hignight was doing and the children told all about their visit, Nancy asked everybody which name they liked best for a blue jay: Tillie or Sapphire.

Almost everyone said Sapphire.

3
SHOOTING MARBLES
(WHY PLOWING ONIONS WAS FUN)

When they stayed for a few days with their cousins, Frankie, Nancy and Rose were, naturally, expected to help with the chores—and there were what seemed endless rows of onions to plow! The children had to push a big, and quite heavy, garden plow along both sides of each row. The mountain dirt was full of rocks—millions of them, Nancy figured. One or two rounds with the plow was about all that any kid could do at one time.

None of them minded the work, though, because while they waited their turn to plow, there was a game called Shooting Marbles! The dusty flat ground in the far corner of the onion patch was perfect for the big circle drawn with a sharp stick. The children sat gathered around the ring, pooling their small marbles in the center of the circle. Each child took a turn with their favorite big shooter marble then, to knock as many of the marbles out of the ring as they could.

Concentration was key as each child made a fist, eyed the marble to be displaced, and then sent their shooter marble flying toward it with a quick flick of the thumb. You got to keep all the marbles you sent out of the ring, and have another turn as long as you were winning marbles. Whoever was plowing would be out that round of play, and if the round of play wasn't finished when they got done plowing that row, they would have to plow one more until it was.

Nancy had collected more marbles than any of the others, but she knew they could all be gone in a day's play, especially when Rose was at her best and had her lucky tiger eye shooter marble.

4

THE OVERALLS

Today, Nancy had once again been declared Marbles champion—this was the third day in a row! She couldn't help feeling prideful of it, and was fairly dancing through the house after the long afternoon of plowing onions and shooting marbles.

Besides winning a beautiful array of marbles, including Helen's favorite purple shooter marble, Nancy had spotted a beautiful sparkly rock while she was walking home from the onion patch, making her day even better. She was on the way to the bedroom to put it, along with the marbles, in her paper sack (which she used in lieu of a suitcase for her clothes on her visits to her grandparents' house).

When Nancy passed through the bathroom, she stopped for a moment, as she always did, to admire the overalls.

In the house, Mama and Papa Apple had a small room everyone called the bathroom. They didn't have indoor plumbing and in fact, few people Nancy knew of did. Maybe Mama Apple had heard of it and meant to have a real bathroom later on. In this 'bathroom,' though, instead of a bathtub or commode, there were shelves and shelves full of neatly stacked overalls! Nancy *loved* seeing those rows of overalls, with all the buckles stuck inside, some dark denim, some faded, and even striped. Girls wore only dresses, but oh, how Nancy longed to try on a pair of those overalls! She never did, though. She just looked at them longingly, then ran on out to play with Rose and the others.

Today, however, in her triumphant mood, Nancy was feeling more than a bit adventurous. She tucked her rock in the marbles bag, which she laid on top of a stack of overalls. Then, she pulled a beautiful pair of softly faded, dusk-blue overalls from the next stack over. When she held up the dungarees in front of her, she could easily see that they were her very size! Nancy took her marbles bag along with the pair of overalls and brazenly walked on to the bedroom. Suppressing a giggle, she imagined Frankie's upcoming reaction to her sister in overalls.

But just as she pulled out her paper sack to pack her marbles bag safely away, she heard Aunt Irene calling for her—"Nancy? Didn't you want to help with the pies?"—and Nancy remembered that she had asked her aunt to show her how she made the fried pies the next time she made them.

Nancy became suddenly shy about the overalls and quickly crammed them into the open sack, along with the bag holding her marbles and sparkly rock. Then she ran to the kitchen and learned how to make fried pies.

Somehow, the overalls in her sack under the bed kept floating to the top of her mind, though.

By the time the fried pies, beautifully folded over, flaky and shiny with buttery crust, were finished, and supper—leftover fried chicken, biscuits and garden vegetables—was on the table, Nancy was beginning to think her idea of taking the overalls to try on was not a good one, after all.

But her main thought was not on the worthiness of the idea, it was how to get the overalls out of the paper sack and back into the bathroom.

She wondered if this was how thieves feel when they sneak things, and then she had a horrible thought: "Jiminy cricket! I *am* a thief!"

Despite her love of fried chicken, Nancy could not manage more than a few bites of supper. Mama Apple noticed and wondered out loud if Nancy was getting something. (There was a stomach bug going around, according to the talk at church.) Nancy forced down some bites of fried potatoes and made herself smile.

"I'm just saving room for the fried pies," she lied, adding to her sin of thievery.

The family went to the front porch after the meal to enjoy their pies, and shell peas in the late evening light. Nancy had no interest in pies, or shelling peas, either, but was resigned to pretending happiness about everything, which was becoming exhausting. But as she started to accept the pie that she didn't want, an idea popped into her head.

"Mama Apple, would you braid my hair!"

Nancy thought she might have interrupted a conversation, by the scowl on Frankie's face and

Aunt Irene's open mouth, but she determinedly held her ground, even pulling her hair back from her face for effect.

Mama Apple kept shelling peas but nodded.

This was going to work, Nancy just knew it.

She trotted into the house, calling "I'll go get my comb, then!"

As you might have guessed, she went straight to the bedroom, retrieved the plundered overalls, and returned them to the bathroom, folded as neatly as she had found them.

Then she raced toward the front door before realizing she had forgotten her comb, so ran back to the bedroom once more, then forced herself to walk slowly out the door to the porch, where Mama Apple was waiting to braid her hair.

"One braid or two?"

"Oh, two, I think," Nancy answered happily. "Hey, Rose, would you please hand me a fried pie?"

Aunt Irene's Fried Pies

INGREDIENTS:

2 c flour	Dash nutmeg
1 t salt	1/2 c shortening
1 t sugar	1 t vinegar
5 T water	

Dried, canned or fresh peaches,
berries, or other fruit

DIRECTIONS:

Combine flour, salt, sugar,
and nutmeg.

Cut in shortening.

Gradually add water and
vinegar with a fork.

Shape dough into a small ball.

Divide into walnut-sized balls.

(over)

Roll each ball
    into a 3 1/2 inch circle.
Place a spoonful of your
    favorite dried, canned, or
    fresh fruit on each circle.
Fold circle in half, using cold water
    to seal the edges together.
Crimp the edges with the tines
    of a fork.
Fry over medium heat in
    1/2 inch of oil, turning once.
When pies are golden brown, remove
    and drain on paper towels.
Sprinkle with powdered sugar.

5

But Joy Comes in the Morning

Some of the best times at Mama and Papa Apple's, for Nancy anyway, came at bedtime! Nancy loved the soft, happy glow the kerosene lamp gave, and she even loved the smell of it. The children could leave the lamp on until Uncle Lee and Aunt Irene came to bed. When they heard Uncle Lee winding the clock, Nancy and the others knew they didn't have much longer until they'd have to lower the wick in the lamp, and their fun would be over. They hurried to fit their games into the little time left.

They made shadows on the wall by the lamplight. They used their hands to resemble animals or anything else they could think of, and whoever guessed what it was got the next turn. One time Rose made a fish using both her hands together and twisting her fingers some way. Nancy didn't know how, but it was very impressive. Everybody saw right away that it was a fish, but Nancy shouted it out first and won.

Her favorite nighttime game, though, was I Spy. One of the bedroom walls was papered with newsprint—the *Kansas City Star* and, of course, the *Rural Record*. They would find a large headline, or advertisement, or something from the Funnies, and describe it. The first one to "spy" it was the winner.

Little GL once spied "S.O.S." All the children looked and looked for that S.O.S. but no one ever did find it, and they finally had to give up. Whoever would have thought to look under the picture of Santa Claus! The letters stood for *Save our Santa*, Nancy discovered, after reading further the next morning.

None of the children ever left the pallet on the floor to go look. The rule was that everyone had to be able to see the thing that was spied from where they were. They could see surprisingly well by the gleam of that small but stalwart kerosene lamp, though, so it was never a problem staying on the pallet to look.

On the night Aunt Irene told the girls they were old enough now to sleep in the front bedroom, in the shiny brass bed, Nancy was delighted. She, along with Frankie, Rose, and Helen, snuggled happily under the pretty blue and yellow checked quilt, talking about the day and planning the tomorrow. There was no newsprint on the wall in this room, so they couldn't play I Spy—Nancy thought that was very unfortunate—and just when they had decided to make shadow figures by the lamplight, they heard Uncle Lee winding the clock and knew they had waited too late. Helen extinguished the oil lamp. The girls whispered together for a little while, then the others, one by one, went to sleep.

Nancy had, of course, heard the word 'lonesome' used before, but that night she learned its true meaning! Everyone in the household except Nancy was asleep. All was quiet in the house. Through the open windows drifted in the night sounds. There were sounds of dry flies, crickets, frogs, and owls... then the sweet little sounds of goat bells and the deeper sounds of cowbells.

Nancy began to wonder how her mother and daddy were doing without her at home. She suddenly felt very sorry for her parents because they were alone.

Tears began flooding, but she made sure no noise came out in case someone heard her, because then they would be sad, too.

Daylight made all the difference! The smell of Aunt Irene's bacon, birds chirping, her cousins yawning and stretching…Nancy couldn't wait to start another fun-filled day!

As she sat in the pew at church a few weeks later, counting pine knots on the wall while listening vaguely to the preacher, she suddenly sat upright as she heard him read a Bible verse…

"But joy…comes in the morning!" he pronounced.

Nancy immediately thought of that night on the mountain. She didn't hear much else of what he said about it, but from then on, whenever she heard that Bible verse she remembered the feeling of that lonely, sad night followed by joy in the morning, and she thought she knew just how the psalmist felt.

6

LEFT BEHIND

"Uncle Lee, can we get off the wagon when we get to Goat's Bluff?"

"Sure," was his reply.

Nancy and Rose were in the bed of the wagon, surrounded by watermelons, onions, potatoes and corn. Uncle Lee was in charge of transporting the girls to Nancy's house while he peddled the harvest of crops to folks in the valley. Frankie had stayed home to attend Singing School, and although Rose and Nancy hadn't wanted to go to Singing School, they did want to go to see Frankie, as well as some of their friends, perform in the program tomorrow (not to mention, there would be cookies and punch afterwards).

When Uncle Lee went down the mountain, he had to hold the brake on almost the entire time, or else the wagon would bump up against the horses and hurt or scare them. It was slow going, and the kids liked to hop off the wagon to play sometimes. They easily caught up with the wagon to jump back on when they got tired of playing.

Nancy and Rose already knew exactly where they wanted to get off to play this time. On the way up the mountain a week ago, they had climbed down the rocks of Goat's Bluff to splash in the stream there. It had been a wonderful place to wade, all crystal-clear and shaded; also, they had seen crawdads, which were fun to catch. You had to be careful that they didn't pinch you when you grabbed them, but then again, that was the fun part about it.

Nancy was so intent on the story Rose was telling her, though, that they almost missed their jumping-off spot.

Henry, Rose told her, had gotten loose one time in the house in the middle of the night. (Nancy remembered that Charles used to have a flying squirrel for a pet, but she had never heard this particular story about Henry, who had been well-known for getting into mischief.) Rose had just gotten to the part about Mama Apple coming, yawning, into the kitchen after hearing a loud noise, to see Henry sitting on the table holding a piece of huckleberry pie in his claws. Nancy gasped in delight at the thought, then noticed that they had almost missed Goat's Bluff. She elbowed Rose to get her attention and they quickly hopped out of the wagon.

They didn't see any crawdads until they began turning over the rocks at the bottom of the crystalline pool of water. The little creatures came skittering out, annoyed at having been disturbed. The girls skillfully grabbed a few in turn, to admire, then let them go back to their hiding places.

Rose spotted a long mossy-green log floating nearby, which they decided to pretend was an alligator, prodding it with a stick and then running away screaming as it moved in the water. They took turns saving each other from it for a while, then Rose suggested they climb the rocks of the bluff.

Nancy thought they should turn this into a game

by seeing who could make it up the hill first each time, and that turned out to be a lot of fun…so much fun, in fact, that the cousins and best friends almost forgot they had a wagon to catch up with.

"Um, Rose, don't you think we'd better go get back on the wagon now?"

Nancy could tell by the look on Rose's face that she had pretty much forgotten, too. Rose started right away to put her shoes back on, even though she didn't say anything.

Nancy put her shoes on, as well, and they hurried up the cliff and started down the road. Nancy didn't see the wagon and horses at all.

"Rooose…" Nancy ventured quietly… "Uncle Lee wouldn't leave us, would he?"

Rose said right away, "Of course not! But…he *did* know we jumped out of the wagon, didn't he?"

Nancy went over and over it in her mind. Uncle Lee had said "sure," after all, when she'd asked him. But that was early this morning.

Nancy began to think about how she and Rose would survive all alone at Goat's Bluff on the mountain. They could get water from the stream to drink. What would they eat, though? Nancy remembered seeing some muscadine vines, but they

would still get hungry with just berries to eat. They didn't have anything to build a fire with, even if they could catch a fish somehow. Also, where would they sleep?

Nancy felt tears sliding down her face. She pretended to fix her shoe so that Rose wouldn't see. Even though they *were* best friends and cousins, Nancy didn't want Rose to know she was being a crybaby. But Nancy guessed she knew anyway, because Rose put her arm around her cousin and gave her a hug.

"Come on, Nancy. You know as well as I do that Uncle Lee would never leave us. Now…let's go catch that wagon!"

Nancy was beginning to get a stich in her side from running, when Rose spotted the tiny speck that was Uncle Lee and the wagon. It was far, far down the mountain still, but the girls slowed down to a walk, since things didn't seem *quite* as dismal, and Nancy's side was hurting.

They walked a little, then ran a little, then walked a little, then ran a little, then walked a little, then ran a little, then walked a little more, then ran a little more, then finally caught up to the wagon and hopped on.

Uncle Lee asked mildly, "You girls have a good time at Goat's Bluff?"

They never did tell him they had been worried that he might have left them, and as far as Nancy knew, he never found out about it.

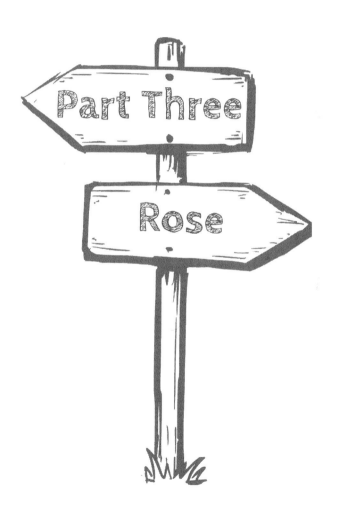

Part Three

Rose

1

GL PLANTS WATERMELON SEEDS

Rose saw the two of them while she was walking in from the onion field. GL had a huge smile on his face as he stepped alongside Papa Apple, kneeling to drop the watermelon seeds one at a time into the ground and then covering them with a little dirt the way his grandfather had shown him.

Rose was stirring the potatoes, which were beginning to brown nicely in the frypan, when GL came in from planting the melon seeds, asking if he could ring the dinner bell. Mama Apple told him yes, he could, but that it wasn't time yet. Grandma was just putting her hands in to mix up the biscuit dough in her big blue mixing bowl, so Rose knew it would be a while yet.

Aunt Irene turned to tell GL to please run down to the spring to get some butter to have with dinner. Rose knew her aunt meant Rose too when she said it, because GL wasn't allowed to go by himself to the spring, ordinarily. Mama Apple handed GL, and Rose too, a teacake, to help with the wait for dinner, and they munched their thin brown cookies while they walked to the spring for the butter.

The spring was where Mama and Papa Apple kept their milk, butter, watermelons, and anything else that needed to stay cold—under the chill of the cold spring water. One of the kids was generally sent to retrieve whatever was needed.

"Brrr," Rose muttered as she reached her arm into the chilly water to grab the bucket that held the butters and cheeses. She pried off the lid, took one of the butter mounds, wrapped tightly in brown paper, and turned to hand it to GL to carry home— she knew he always wanted to carry it.

GL, however, was crouched down dropping what looked to be a seed into the ground. He jumped up, stepped three exaggerated steps, and repeated the process.

When he saw Rose, with her hand on her hip watching him, GL said, "I'm planting watermelons!

You want to help me cover up my watermelon seeds?"

With one hand holding the butter, Rose clapped her other hand over her mouth with a gasp.

"GL! You can't…it's…*no, no, GL!*" she finally said, lacking words in her surprise.

GL continued taking melon seeds from his pockets and distributing them.

"GL! You are wasting those, and Grandpa is going to be very upset! Now stop that this minute," Rose said sternly, more suitable words coming to her now.

GL's pockets were now empty, so he had to stop anyway, but Rose's words (the more suitable ones) were starting to sink in. He began to cover the seeds up hurriedly, glancing around, Rose supposed, to make sure Grandpa wasn't watching.

Rose knew, though, that Grandpa almost never came to the spring unless maybe he was bringing a couple of watermelons to chill. And, she thought wryly, the watermelon seeds had just now been planted, so that wouldn't be the case.

Rose threw her hands in the air in exasperation at her young cousin, then handed him the butter to carry home.

GL handed the butter mound back to her as they walked, then reached to hold hands with his older and wiser cousin, marching them along humming a song Grandpa had taught him. Rose slowed him down to a walk but found herself feeling more patient, so she tried to explain to GL how watermelon seeds have to have a lot of sunlight to grow, and wouldn't come up at the shady spring.

She wasn't sure he was even listening, though, because he kept humming that song.

2
THE SPRING

The children went to the spring often in the summer. Just a short walk down the hill from the house, the cold spring was a perfect respite from the heat after chores on those long sun-filled days. It was a made-to-order play spot.

When the cousins were all there, Rose always suggested they plant flowers at the spring. This project began with making a dam. Rose, Nancy and Charles would lift huge rocks around the spring, carry them to the water and lower them in. Rose liked the invincible feeling of being strong enough to lift the boulders, as they called them. Then, all the children picked wildflowers along the bank of the spring and planted the colorful array of blossoms around the big rocks to create their masterpiece. Later in the afternoon, or sometimes the next day, they lifted the rocks out so the spring could keep going where it wanted, but they never minded the extra work—it was enough to have made their pretty garden by the rocks in the spring.

Rose's favorite game to play in the icy spring water was what they called hopping the rocks. It was played this way: Everyone in the game lined up to hop from rock to rock in the water. The winner was the one who got the farthest without falling off or touching a foot to the water. Nimble-Foot Nancy, as Uncle Lee called her sometimes—Rose guessed because she was good at races and such—was best at the game, but tiny GL showed amazing promise. He would skip over those rocks like it was the easiest thing in the world. When he would eventually slip on a patch of moss and fall knees-first into the water, he'd jump up laughing at himself, despite the bruises and occasional cut from a sharp rock. But he couldn't beat Nancy or Rose—not yet, anyway.

3

Baby Goats

eeeuck!"

Charles had an awful expression on his face when he swallowed the cod liver oil that Aunt Irene spooned determinedly into his mouth. Rose scrunched her eyes and nose up like his and could almost taste that awful stuff herself, just from watching him.

Charles had woken up through the night hot, then cold, and he didn't want to get out of bed or eat breakfast this morning. Rose and her cousins had pitched in to do his chores before devouring ham and biscuits, gravy and eggs, while Charles slept through it all.

After Nancy had washed the dishes while Rose dried and Frankie put them away, they had decided to ask Aunt Irene if they could go play with the baby goats.

And there they found her in the bedroom giving Charles his yucky medicine. Charles looked sadder than ever when he discovered they were going out to see the goats.

Yesterday the children had all claimed one of the little goat kids for their own. Charles had chosen the smallest one and had named it Alfie. Rose knew there was nothing he'd rather be doing, if he wasn't so tired and cold, than going out to the hillside with them to see Alfie right now.

"We'll check on Alfie for you," Frankie was assuring Charles.

That's when Rose got what she knew right away was the perfect idea.

As soon as they were outside the bedroom, she whispered the plan. Frankie, Nancy and Helen readily agreed, but Helen said they had to ask her mother first. Frankie, Nancy and Rose all said that yes, of course they would.

Aunt Irene smiled and said it would be all right.

Thus, the cousins headed out to find Alfie, to

carry the little goat inside to see Charles to cheer him up!

When they topped the grassy green knoll, the goats came running to see them. Sure enough, all their baby goats were there.

Baby goats are way more fun than any dolls, Rose thought to herself, as she picked her goat kid up and cuddled her lovingly.

Rose told the tiny goat that her name was Tina. The baby goat stared right at Rose's face with her big round eyes, as if she liked the name. Rose stroked Tina's softness for a minute, then she set Tina down and watched Frankie, Helen and Nancy find their babies.

But when Frankie bent down happily to pick up the small goat she had claimed as her own, Tina locked eyes on Frankie's behind and promptly set out at a run. Rose could only gasp as Tina charged her tiny horns right into Frankie's outstretched bottom and knocked her over!

Frankie sat up with such a surprised face that the other girls couldn't help themselves, they started laughing. It turned into one of those times where you try to stop laughing, then you look at each other and just start laughing again. They finally plopped down on the ground to catch their breath, the goats looking at them curiously, wondering, Rose guessed, what these strange human antics meant.

GL was coming up the hill to join them, and when he heard what had happened, he howled with laughter, too. Even Frankie, who had been scowling throughout, began to giggle.

All the girls said they could hardly believe the baby goat was that strong… "and ornery, too," said GL, and they all started laughing again.

It was Nancy who remembered the plan, and Rose felt a little guilty because she had been having so much fun, she'd almost forgotten about poor Charles, and how they were going to take him his goat to cheer him up.

Rose had to admit that she had been a little jealous when Charles had called Alfie for his, because that teeny goat sure was cute, and it was the most playful one, too, chasing Charles and then turning to let Charles chase him, and following him wherever he went.

But, of course, Charles wasn't there now because he was too tired and cold, so the children looked around for Alfie to take to him. But Alfie was nowhere to be seen! They walked all over the hillside looking and calling his name. The goats followed them, bleating as if they were trying to help, and Rose thought maybe they were. But Alfie didn't come, and they got more and more worried.

After a long time of walking and hollering "Al-fieee, Al-fieee!" Frankie voiced what Rose knew they all had been thinking.

"Remember that bobcat that Papa Apple said he heard in the woods last week? What if it got Alfie!"

Rose felt as sad then, after she let that thought sit in her head, as Charles had looked in his bed.

But Charles looking sad seemed a long, long time ago, instead of just a little while earlier. They had all been happy then with their thoughts of cheering him up with little Alfie, and now Alfie… Well, Rose just couldn't let herself think it anymore. She made herself keep walking and shouting for Alfie, and the others started walking and shouting again, too, but with sad, worried looks on their faces that Rose knew were reflected on her face, as well. There was an awful feeling in her stomach to match her worried face, and when she started thinking about telling Charles that a bobcat got Alfie, her stomach started to feel worse.

All the children shouted Alfie's name for a long

time, and the goats bleated all around them. They
walked around the hillside back and forth, and
back and forth until Helen suggested they might as
well stop looking and go tell Charles the sad news.
Rose didn't think they should tell him, though, and
Nancy and Frankie agreed with her. They were
discussing this, and trying to decide if they should
or not, when GL stopped completely still with a
shout.

"*Alfie? Alfie! It…it's Alfie!*"

GL was staring at the barn and pointing. The
cousins stopped and—far, far up on the roof of
Grandma and Grandpa's barn? There was Alfie!

"Look, he's proud of himself!" Rose told her
cousins.

She didn't know how that littlest kid had climbed
all the way up there, but they were all so relieved
that a bobcat hadn't got him that she and the others
didn't even wonder about it very much. When Alfie
saw them coming closer, he ambled to the edge of
the roof and jumped right down, landing on his
tiny feet and running to join them! Rose picked
him up, and they took Alfie straight to Charles,
who seemed very much cheered up to see him.

When Uncle Lee took Rose home the next day,

though, she started to feel tired and cold, then hot, then cold again. Two days later her cheeks got very puffy and red, and her mother said she had caught the mumps from Charles. GL and Helen, and Frankie and Nancy, all got the mumps that week, too! Rose wished she had someone to bring her baby goat to her, while she lay there all tired and sick.

But she knew that Charles, who was almost well by then, would take good care of Tina and Alfie, and the other goat kids, until the cousins were together again.

4

THE SECRET

Rose had recovered from the mumps, as had Helen, Charles and GL, and she could hardly wait to get to her grandparent's house to see her cousins. Because of those stupid mumps, she had had to stay in the house for almost two weeks now. She was more than ready for some fun and adventure! Frankie and Nancy wouldn't be there today, her mother had told her; Aunt Phoebe thought they might still be contagious. Rose didn't know what difference that would make, since all the kids had *had* the mumps now, but maybe the grown-ups could get them, she guessed. Did grown-ups get mumps? Rose was about to ask her mother but then saw that they had arrived, and forgot all about her question.

Rose jumped from the wagon even before the horses had come to a stop, prompting a frown from her daddy and a gasp from her mother. Rose landed on her feet and ran toward the front porch, where she saw Uncle Lee waving to her. She scanned the porch for Helen, then slowed to a walk as she and her cousin made eye contact.

Uncle Lee had a watermelon ready to slice open on the porch, so Rose made her way to Helen's side to wait for the melon to be cut.

Helen had a secret.

Rose could tell that she did, because she kept grinning, then laughing for no reason that Rose could see, and then smiling, rather smugly, again.

In fact, she could tell that Helen was just about to bust, wanting to tell her something.

Rose and Helen finished their watermelon at almost exactly the same time, and both politely refused a second slice.

"What is it!" Rose demanded as they cleared the porch.

"Weeeell...you know how Mother has a birthday this week..."

Rose hadn't known that, but said yes anyway, to keep the conversation going.

Helen beamed as she announced, "I have found the *perfect* present."

Helen went on to explain that while on the way to Myrtle and Claud Hignight's house yesterday, she and Charles had taken a shortcut through the brush and found the most enormous patch of huckleberry bushes she had ever seen. And her mother, she told Rose, had been complaining that she didn't have enough huckleberries this week to even make a pie. Helen's idea was simple but genius: They would take the washtub there and fill it up with huckleberries for Aunt Irene!

Since Charles knew about the berry bushes, and also because it would be good to have some help, the girls decided to let him in on the plan. Charles, as they had known he would, thought it was a great idea and wondered why he hadn't thought of it himself.

The washtub was so big that the children had to carry it with one person on each side. It was rather hard going through the dense forest with that big tub between them, over hills and rocks on the thin trail to the place Helen had discovered. That might

have given them pause for thought about this mission, but all the children could see was Helen's mother's shining eyes as she saw the marvelous gift they would present to her.

The huckleberry bushes must have covered an acre or more! Why, it was a whole *orchard* of huckleberry bushes, Rose thought in amazement. They began picking right away. Those were the plumpest, most perfect berries anyone ever saw. But the children didn't even eat very many, so intent they were on the job at hand.

An hour or so later, their backs ached, and their hands were purple. When Rose looked up, she saw only purple for several seconds. The washtub wasn't full like they had planned, with the berries just going up about halfway, but they decided that would still make the most amazing present ever. Rose grabbed the handle on one side while Helen grabbed the other...and found it so heavy they could hardly lift it! Charles rushed over to try, but he fared no better.

There was no way that they were going to leave a single berry behind. The valiant children took turns, two at a time, hefting the washtub of huckleberries back to Mama and Papa Apple's.

When they finally lowered the weighty washtub to its designated hiding place, Rose groaned. Her arms were sore, her neck ached along with her back, and she had blisters on her fingers. Charles and Helen did, too, but the children didn't complain to anyone. (How could they, without giving it away!) They kept their secret, hiding that washtub with the birthday present for Aunt Irene in it behind a hay bale in the barn, until the next morning.

When they carried the washtub to the house and presented it to Aunt Irene early the next day, she was very, very happy and hugged them all. She couldn't believe, she said, that they did all that work for her birthday.

Later, though, Rose wondered if her aunt was really that happy or maybe pretending a little bit, because Aunt Irene was canning huckleberries for all the rest of that week, and the next week, too. And that, Rose knew, was a lot of work. But every time Rose came through the kitchen, her aunt was humming or singing while she canned, so maybe she was.

5

GL's Watermelon

Much to Rose's relief, Aunt Phoebe had *finally* decided that Frankie and Nancy weren't contagious with the mumps anymore. After hurrying to the barn to show the sisters how much their baby goats had grown, all the children set off for the spring to play, stopping on the hillside to pull bunches of fresh green onion blades for Charles to carry in his pockets for them to snack on throughout the afternoon.

Arriving at the spring, Nancy was the one who noticed the small green plant with the tiny watermelon on it. GL was pleased to see it, although not a bit surprised, Rose noticed.

Rose pointed out to him that it was growing in a wide place between the trees where sunlight came in, in case he had listened to her that day when she had been patient and explained the part about the sunlight.

The rest of the children *were* surprised, very, but still didn't pay much attention after looking at it and hearing the story of how GL had planted the seeds there.

But, the thing is, in the coming weeks that watermelon grew. It grew…and grew…and grew. It got to where Rose and the others *begged* to go get milk or butter or cheese from the spring for dinner, just to see how big it had gotten. (Aunt Irene felt grateful that she had such helpful children, to ask to run errands for her like that.)

In fact, the watermelon got so big, the children began comparing it with Grandpa's biggest melon in the truck patch of watermelons. GL took it all in stride. He had assumed that big watermelons would come up when he planted the seeds there and was not too awfully concerned now with his watermelon's size… "But Rose, why *wouldn't* it be as big as Grandpa's watermelons?" he had asked her when she was jumping up and down, pointing out the size of it one day.

On the day that it surpassed Grandpa's biggest melon, the children held a discussion. Should GL fess up to Grandpa about the watermelon seeds he'd planted not in the watermelon patch, so that he could show Grandpa the big, big watermelon—or not? Of course, it was ultimately GL's choice, Rose knew.

GL surprised them all with his decision, though. The day the kids held the discussion about telling or not telling Grandpa was the day before the day before Independence Day—the Fourth of July, Uncle Lee called it. Their aunts and uncles and cousins always came on that day, and after a big dinner, Grandpa would cut the biggest watermelon in the watermelon patch. And, the day after the day after the discussion they'd had, GL proudly walked into the kitchen while the family was sitting down to breakfast, *lugging his watermelon!*

Everyone stopped pulling out their chairs to sit down, or pouring their milk, or talking to each other, and just stared.

Grandpa said to him, "Why, GL, how come you

to be in the melon patch this time of day? I believe you picked the best one, though."

Rose had to work hard, then, at being quiet and not telling it all herself. She knew it was GL's story, but it was still hard.

When GL told them how it was his own watermelon he had planted down by the spring, Uncle Lee and Aunt Irene and Grandma and Grandpa were amazed. GL said he wanted his watermelon to be the one cut open for Independence Day.

That evening after the children lit firecrackers that Uncle Frank had brought, and the grown-ups played horseshoes, Grandpa cut open GL's watermelon. Rose believed it was just as good-tasting as any she'd eaten.

And GL never did get in trouble, although Rose saw Grandpa talking to him—real serious-looking—under the big oak tree. GL was nodding his head just as solemnly, so she thought he might have got a talking-to, but he didn't get a whipping, anyway.

6

MOTHER KNOWS BEST

"Rose, tell me about when you were my age and you went in the goose pen…please?"

GL was helping Rose lay goose feathers in the sun to dry. This morning Aunt Irene and Grandma had pulled the soft little feathers, the ones on the undersides, from the geese, and Rose's job was to spread them carefully in the hot sun. This dried them and also made them free of germs. They repeated the process every time the geese grew more of those tiny, soft feathers. After the feathers had been in the sun a long time, Aunt Irene put them in a special sack where they were all kept until there were enough for a new pillow or a bed.

For a bed, as you might guess, it took a very, very long time to collect enough feathers. Rose had lain on her mother and daddy's new feather bed mattress one time, and it was so cushiony and warm that she'd felt like she was laying on a cloud. She recalled the splendid feeling of sinking down into it with the billowy softness all around her. She had pretended all that evening, until her parents had come to bed, that she was a princess and that was her royal bed.

This time, there weren't enough feathers for a bed. There were almost enough feathers, though, Aunt Irene had mused this morning, to make Grandma a new pillow. She had even cut out the piece of ticking material for the pillow and sewed all around the edges of the sides to have it ready to fill with the tiny soft feathers. Luckily, Aunt Irene had a sewing machine, called a treadle, that she could use. Otherwise, it would have been much more work, because the stitches had to be very close together so that the feathers wouldn't work their way out.

GL took pride in his work spreading feathers, arranging them on the large rock from smallest to largest, and Rose smiled at this as she began her story.

Although GL was five years old now, Rose still

started the tale like she always had, even though she had just turned four when it happened: "Well, GL, when I was your age…"

The memories came flooding back as Rose related the day she learned a lesson from the geese.

* * *

"Now, Rose, you can play out here in the yard while Mommy goes to the barn to milk the cows, but don't go into the goose pen. Those geese will peck you…*ouch!*" her mother added as emphasis.

"Look, you can swing on the tire swing," she went on.

Rose was four years old, and had learned just recently to hoist herself up on the wood plank hanging from the oak tree to gently swing it back and forth.

Rosa, her mother, went on to the barn with her bucket. Rose waited until her mother was all the way in the barn before she headed straight to the goose pen. Tiny Rose reached up to open the gate and made her way to the geese, who were sitting placidly in the sun.

"I don't even know what I had planned to do

when I got in there, maybe try to pet them or pick one up. I just knew going in there was forbidden so it must be something fun," Rose explained to GL...

The biggest goose looked up. Rose and the goose locked eyes, then within the very next second, all those mild-mannered geese were marching toward her, squawking and hissing and flapping their wings. Rose was too surprised to even cry out as they came closer and closer.

She fleetingly thought to herself, *"Why are they so mad at **me**?"* Then suddenly she was being *pinched* all over by this army of geese! Rose let out a shriek and tried to run, but the outraged geese kept pinching her with their beaks and flogging her with their wings.

"Then, as if from out of nowhere, Mommy was there! She swooped me up and carried me out of that goose pen and sat me on the ground!"

GL's eyes were large as he stopped laying feathers down, to take it in. "And that is the day I learned," Rose finished, "that Mother knows best!" (Rose thought it was nice to end a story with a moral.)

"That was when Mother and Daddy and I lived here on the mountain with Grandma and Grandpa, like you do now, GL. We moved to our own house later that year. I'm sure glad it's closeby, though."

"Me, too," said GL, and Rose knew he meant it.

Epilogue

Too soon, August was drawing to a close. School began next week. All the children had new Blue Horse writing tablets, and long new pencils their daddies had sharpened with their pocketknives; and they were happy at the thought of seeing their friends and meeting their new teachers. Still, though, Frankie, Nancy and Rose were reluctant to leave their grandparent's house.

When it was time to head down the mountain to their homes, Frankie, Nancy and Rose said an almost teary good-bye to their cousins, hugged the grown-ups, and promised they'd be back when school let out in October for Harvest time. Those three weeks in October, when the children would help with the fall harvest of crops and making the sorghum molasses, seemed a very long time away, though. Rose and Nancy lingered as long as possible, holding hands until time to climb up and into the wagons to start the journeys to their homes.

* * *

Tucked into her feather bed at her house at Shoal Creek, Rose asked sleepily, "Can we go help when Grandpa makes molasses?"

"Of course," her mother replied, "but the sugarcane won't be ready for a long while yet!"

"I know. But don't you wish it was tomorrow?"

That same evening, finally snuggled in their bed after the long ride home, Nancy whispered to Frankie, "I still think I could have beat Helen, if I'd just had my lucky shooter."

"Don't tell me you're still thinking about that marbles game!" Frankie groaned.

"Well, I am, and I could have...do you think that new baby goat will remember me?"

At this, Frankie smiled.

"I think so," she yawned. "And maybe you'll beat Helen, too, if you—" Frankie began, but Nancy was already sound asleep.

Frankie snuggled deeper under the familiar quilt, and while she became sleepier and sleepier, she thought of all the things they would do the next time…the next time Frankie, Nancy and Rose were with their cousins on the mountain.

Top left (left to right): Frank, Phoebe, Frankie and Nancy Apple

Top right: Mama and Papa Apple (Will and Cordelia Apple) Nancy and Frankie called their grandparents Mama Apple and Papa Apple, while the rest of the grandchildren called them Grandma and Grandpa.

Phoebe Apple always pointed out this one-room school and church house to Frankie and Nancy on their way. It is called the Liberty School and Church, and still stands there today. (Photo by Alan Wagoner)

*Below:
Charles*

Their horses, Tipper and Dollie, took Frankie
and Nancy's family safely to Mama and Papa
Apple's each time they went.

Frankie and Nancy liked to get out to play in the water at Shoal Creek.
(Photo by Denver Dennis)

Left: Milk, butter, and cheese were kept in a bucket under the cold water of the spring.
(Photo by Karen Westmoreland Townsend)

Center: GL

Bottom: Helen with the goats at Mama and Papa Apple's farm.

Frankie and Nancy saw the newly built Spring Lake dam as they went to Mama and Papa Apple's. The lake and dam continue to be a popular attraction to this day.
(Photo by Nathaniel Metzer)

Nancy and Rose were afraid they had been left behind at Goat's Bluff.
(Photo by Walter Gorman)

If you enjoyed *Frankie, Nancy and Rose on the Mountain*, you may enjoy *Charles, GL and Helen on the Mountain*, coming soon!

From *Charles, GL and Helen on the Mountain*:

HELEN'S TREASURE

"Mother! Look what I *found!*"

Helen had run straight to the house after her discovery, almost tripping on the top step as she bounded onto the porch. She slowed then, knowing that her beautiful find might have been broken into a million pieces, had she fallen down those steps.

Grandpa had recently made a deal with the folks in the kitchen at the Mount Magazine lodge, to haul away their barrels of scraps, in turn for Helen's family using them for the hogs to eat. Helen's job being to feed the hogs, she had to admit she had grumbled a bit when she had dragged the smelly barrel from the wagon to the hog pen that day.

Helen most assuredly was not complaining now!

As she had emptied that barrel—yes, with the stinky, disgusting garbage—a delicate, exquisite, *beautiful* china plate had come tumbling out! (A fork fell out, too, but Helen paid no attention to it, so excited she was about the china.)

More from instinct than thought, Helen took off running for the house, clutching the tiny plate tightly in her hand.

Having heard her daughter's shouts, Irene stood at the front door waiting for her, hoping she didn't have need to go get the hoe to kill a rattlesnake.

"Well, my goodness!"

Helen could tell she was very surprised, even though, naturally, her mother didn't shout and take off running, as had been Helen's reaction. Irene told her that they would wash the china and return it to the people at the lodge.

Helen carefully washed and dried the treasure, then set it on top of the warmer oven so that she could take it down to admire from time to time.

Do you know, the next week when Lee Apple

took that beautiful plate back to the lodge, they said that he didn't have to bring things like that back, and to just to keep whatever fell into the slop barrels!

From then on, not only did Helen not mind feeding the hogs, she could *hardly wait*, and she usually found at least one treasure each time she emptied the barrel from the lodge kitchen.

She kept them all—cups, plates, saucers, even a butter dish. Some were chipped, but Helen didn't care. Each one was wrapped carefully in brown paper, after she washed it, of course, and placed into the cardboard box holding her collection, which she kept in the Tator House behind the cream separator.

Author's Note

WHEN HELEN was grown up with children of her own, that beautiful lodge burned to the ground. People from the surrounding area were all very sad that nothing from the lodge was saved in the fire's destruction. Helen still had her pretty china that had come from there, though, and when a new lodge was erected, she donated a place setting of it, as well as the butter dish, which can today be seen inside a glass case in the Mt. Magazine Visitors Center.

About the Author

 **GAYLA MCBRIDE EDWARDS** grew up at the foot of Mt. Magazine. She now lives in Fort Smith, Arkansas with her husband Jim, and their two dogs and two cats. She teaches Gifted and Talented Education nearby in Hackett, Arkansas. Her passion is keeping alive the culture, heritage and stories of rural Arkansas.

About the Illustrator

As a professional children's illustrator, **VIKTORIIA DAVYDOVA** has done illustrations for children's and young adult books published worldwide. Her greatest passion is creating fairytale worlds, turning authors' words into images.

Reviews

"Reading this book was akin to traveling through time and being a witness to the scenes as they played out. It was packed with Arkansas cultural history and life lessons learned at young ages. In an era where we need to teach our young people about cultural roots and the value of history, this book comes just at the right time."

–Karen Grady, Gifted and Talented Education Specialist

"This endearing look into the lives of the Apple children gives a glimpse of the beauty of the mountain and the simple pleasures enjoyed by children who fashioned their own fun with imagination and ingenuity. As a descendant of the Rogers family who homesteaded and lived on the east side of the mountain near the one room schoolhouse and church mentioned in the story, I loved picturing the journey past Spring Lake, the Gum Tree and the slippery rocks of Shoal Creek. Even the long trip to the mailbox was typical, although I never walked it. It brings back memories to those of us who enjoyed similar times with grandparents and cousins. This book enlightens those who read it today, giving insight into what formed those who went before us."

–Mabel Faye Rogers Coleman

"In today's busy world it is often difficult to find extra time to sit down and begin reading a good book. By the second page—I was hitching up Tipper and Dollie! A new author, Gayla McBride Edwards, was about to take me on a trip to Mt. Magazine, Arkansas. This journey found me barefoot, energetic and again looking at the world through the eyes of a child. It is quite amazing the way an earthy story, from days gone by, can paint a picture so vividly. It makes one step right into a cold, mountain stream or feel the warmth one feels when thinking about petting their favorite baby goat. This journey will take today's children back in time to the warmhearted and fun-loving simplicity of this family who lived on a Magazine Mountain homestead. I enjoyed the trip and I think you will too!"

–Sharon J. Beard, Author of Koke Goes to Oklahoma,
Raven Goes to Arkansas, Down by the Barn,
and Like a Panther in the Night

"An entertaining and informative story of family relationships and growing up in the Ozark mountains during the Depression years."

–Dr. Curtis Varnell, Social Studies Education Specialist
and author of In the Shadow of the Mountain